United Pan Alta

UNITED PAN ALTA

A Fair and Integrated Northeast Asia

KYOUNGJOO CHA

Author of The Architecture of Fairness

First Edition, 2026
Architecture Press LLC

United Pan Alta: A Fair and Integrated Northeast Asia

Published by
Architecture Press LLC, New York

First Edition, 2026
First Printing: May 2026
ISBN: 979-8-9951139-0-4 (Paperback)
Library of Congress Control Number: 2026905739

Printed in the United States of America

Table of Contents

PREFACE

It took fifty-three years to write this book.

The concept was born in 1973.

The world you are holding is the result.

This work is intentionally concise. It is not a comprehensive history, nor a political program.

It is a structural reflection.

This book began with a question.

In the early 1970s, South Korea was a small, poor, and divided country, positioned at the edge of larger powers and governed under military rule. As a young student, I was among those who participated actively in the political movements for democracy — with urgency, and with conviction.

Yet alongside that struggle, another question remained unresolved:

> *What direction should a divided and vulnerable society take to participate meaningfully in the coming millennium?*

That question could not be answered by opposition alone.

During those years, many ideas were explored — political, religious, ideological, and philosophical. Activists, religious leaders, professors, and thinkers offered guidance. I sought answers from historians, philosophers, and leaders of social movements. None addressed the deeper structural problem: how a small nation, shaped by division and history, could secure both prosperity and freedom in a world dominated by larger systems.

Over time, one conclusion emerged with clarity: the repeated failures of Northeast Asian unification across two thousand years shared a single root cause.

Unfairness.

Every attempt — whether through conquest, empire, or coercion — had been built on structures of domination rather than balance. They failed not from lack of ambition or power, but because no dominated people can sustain participation in a system that extracts from them without reciprocity.

If unfairness was the consistent cause of failure, then the answer was not a new political will or a stronger alliance. It required something more fundamental: a structural architecture of fairness built into the foundation of any new regional framework.

United Pan Alta grew from that realization.

It did not begin as a political project or a call for unification. It began as a search for a structural direction — one that would allow societies of different sizes, histories, and capacities to coexist, cooperate, and remain free. The concept took shape in 1973. It was drawn first as a line on a map of Northeast Asia, discussed with students and professors, and met not with opposition but with quiet encouragement to continue.

Over the decades that followed, the question did not change.

Only the world around it did.

When no existing answer is sufficient, the search itself becomes responsibility.

United Pan Alta proceeds from the premise that regions, like civilizations, are shaped by underlying geographic and historical architectures. When structures fall out of alignment with reality, instability follows. When they realign, new possibilities emerge.

The purpose of this book is limited.

It seeks only to indicate a direction — a small arrow mark suggesting that Northeast Asia may, over time, find coherence through balance rather than domination.

Whether that direction becomes a shared future rests with coming generations.

Why This Book Is Written in English

This book is written in English not because English is the language of Northeast Asia.

It is not.

English is chosen because it is currently the closest approximation to a shared conceptual language across the five nodes of the Pan Alta world. A researcher in Ulaanbaatar, a student in Busan, an engineer in Vladivostok, a policy reader in Tokyo, and a young entrepreneur in Shenyang may share no spoken language between them.

But they may share English.

A vision that cannot cross language cannot cross borders.

This is not a permanent condition. Future generations may find other shared languages — digital, visual, or yet undefined. For now, English serves as the medium through which the framework is offered, not as a cultural preference, but as a structural practicality.

The ideas in this book belong to no single language. They are offered in English so they may travel.

To the Current and Coming Digital Generation

Every generation inherits a world it did not design.

But the current and coming digital generation inherits something no prior generation has encountered: a world already structurally connected — not by treaties, not by empires, not by shared religion — but by technology.

A young person in Seoul and a young person in Tokyo today may never have met. Yet they have played the same games, used the same platforms, purchased from the same digital marketplaces, and consumed the same content — often simultaneously, often without awareness of the border between them.

This is not trivial.

What previous centuries required armies and dynasties to attempt, technology has begun quietly, without permission.

This generation did not ask for this connectivity. It arrived as the condition of their world. What they do with it — whether they recognize it as a structural reality and act with awareness, or treat it as entertainment and ignore its architecture — will determine more about the future of Northeast Asia than any political agreement signed by governments.

United Pan Alta was not written for governments.

It was written for those who will outlive the governments currently in power — and who will one day decide, perhaps without realizing it, what kind of region they inhabit.

The most consequential decisions are often not recognized as decisions at all.

This book asks the digital generation to recognize theirs.

If this work clarifies the region's long-term architecture in the new millennium, it will have fulfilled its role.

—✦—

Kyoungjoo Cha
New York, 2026

How to Read This Book

This book is written for those who believe that the future of Northeast Asia must be prepared before it can be built.

It is not a political proposal.
It is not a prediction.
It is not a call for immediate action.

It is a civilizational guide.

What This Book Is

This book is a blueprint for a long-term vision called *United Pan Alta*—a fair path toward Northeast Asian unity.

It is written to:

provide a shared conceptual framework across borders,

and serve as a durable reference text for current and future generations.

It is meant to be:

- read more than once
- quoted in discussion
- returned to when clarity is needed

This book does not ask readers to agree.
It asks them to understand.

What This Book Is Not

This book is not:

- a manifesto
- an ideology
- a political program
- a geopolitical strategy

- a challenge to existing nation-states

It does not propose:

- borders
- institutions
- enforcement mechanisms
- timelines

A vision imposed by urgency collapses.
A vision prepared with patience endures.

How to Use This Book

Each chapter is written to stand on its own.
Readers may begin anywhere.

Some will read it sequentially.
Others will return only to certain chapters.
Both approaches are valid.

Key ideas are intentionally stated clearly and repeatedly, so they may be:

- cited
- debated
- reinterpreted by future generations

This book is not a command.
It is a compass.

To the Reader

The responsibility for the future does not belong to one generation alone.

This book is written for:

- the current generation, who must prepare
- the next generation, who must decide

History does not reward those who act first.
It rewards those who prepare best.

A Note for the Digital Generation
Reading in the Digital Era

This book was written to be read on paper.

But it will also be read on screens — in fragments, across interrupted sessions, on devices that compete for attention with everything else the digital world offers simultaneously.

Both are valid.

A book that can only be read in silence and sequence has already limited its reach.

The digital generation reads differently — not with less depth, but with different rhythm. They move between sources. They highlight and share single sentences. They return to specific passages weeks or months later, prompted by a conversation or a current event that made an earlier idea suddenly relevant.

This book is designed to survive that kind of reading.

Each chapter stands alone. Key ideas are stated clearly and repeated intentionally — not as redundancy, but as anchors that hold their meaning whether encountered in sequence or in isolation.

Stable ideas do not require continuous reading to remain coherent.

On Sharing and Quoting

In the digital era, a book lives not only on shelves but in the passages, people choose to share.

Readers are encouraged to quote this book — in conversations, in posts, in academic work, in debate. The definitions in the Glossary are intentionally fixed precisely so they remain accurate when quoted out of context. A shared sentence from this book should mean the same thing in isolation as it does within its chapter.

What can be quoted accurately can travel further than what must be read in full.

If a single sentence from this book reaches someone who would never have read the whole — and if that sentence is structurally sound — it has served its purpose.

Why Stable Definitions Matter in a Fast World

The digital world moves quickly. Meanings shift. Words are repurposed, diluted, or weaponized faster than prior generations thought possible.

This is precisely why this book insists on fixed definitions.

In an environment where the same word can mean opposite things on different platforms, a shared conceptual framework becomes more valuable — not less. The Glossary at the front of this book is not academic formality. It is a structural defense against the noise that surrounds every important idea today.

When meanings are stable, conversation becomes possible.
When meanings drift, only volume remains.

The digital generation, more than any before it, understands the cost of unstable language. They have lived inside it. This book offers an alternative — not nostalgia for slower times, but a deliberate architecture of clarity built for fast ones.

Glossary of Core Terms

Pan Alta

A civilizational space defined by long-term geographical, historical, and structural interaction across Northeast Asia.

Pan Alta is not an ethnicity, a nation, or an empire.

It describes a shared reality shaped by land–sea interaction, migration, trade, and coexistence over a few thousand years.

Pan Alta refers to a space of interaction, not an identity.

United Pan Alta

A long-term civilizational vision for Northeast Asia based on fairness, voluntary coordination, and preparation across generations.

It does not propose political unification, territorial change, or institutional authority.

United Pan Alta is a vision for coexistence, not a plan for control.

Fair Path

A non-coercive, preparation-based approach to regional alignment that prioritizes legitimacy, balance, and sustainability over speed or dominance.

A fair path is one that others may choose, not one they are forced to follow.

Fairness

A structural principle by which systems remain stable over time.

Fairness balances interests without domination and enables cooperation without submission.

It precedes stability and legitimacy.

Fairness is not moral preference; it is systemic necessity.

Wealth

The material capacity of a society or region, including:

- economic output
- technological capability
- infrastructure
- energy and resource security

Wealth enables choice but does not guarantee freedom.

Wealth expands what is possible, not what is just.

Freedom

The capacity for sovereign choice, including:

- political self-determination
- cultural continuity
- dignity
- voluntary participation

Freedom without material foundation remains fragile.

Freedom endures only when it is materially supported.

Wealth and Freedom

The dual foundations of a sustainable civilization.

Maximizing one at the expense of the other produces instability.

Long-term systems must expand both simultaneously.

Civilizations fail not from lack of wealth or freedom,
but from the imbalance between them.

Shared Conceptual Framework

A common set of stable definitions and reference concepts that enables cross-border understanding without requiring a shared spoken or written language.

Understanding requires shared meanings, not shared speech.

Preparation

The process by which societies develop intellectual, cultural, and institutional readiness before attempting structural change.

Preparation precedes action and reduces the cost of error.

History rewards preparation more often than ambition.

Unity

A condition of coordination and coexistence achieved without loss of sovereignty, cultural identity, or voluntary choice.

Unity does not require uniformity.

Unity survives when diversity is preserved.

Sovereignty
The right and capacity of a people or state to make independent choices. In the Pan Alta world, sovereignty operates within interdependence, not isolation.
Sovereignty weakens when it denies reality.
Vision
A directional framework that guides preparation without dictating outcomes.
A vision expands the range of possible futures rather than deciding one.
A vision does not command the future; it prepares for it.

Current and Next Generation
The current generation is responsible for preparation.
The next generation is responsible for decision and action.
Those who prepare do not control history,
but they shape the choices history will allow.

Glossary Closing Note
All terms in this glossary are intentionally fixed.
Their meanings do not change throughout this book.
Readers are encouraged to:

- quote them
- debate them
- reinterpret their application

—but not to alter their definitions.
A shared future requires stable words.

—✦—

PART I

Defining the Pan Alta World

Chapter 1 – The Pan Alta World

A Civilizational Definition

"Pan Alta" does not describe an ethnicity.
It does not describe a nation.
It does not describe an empire.

Pan Alta describes a civilizational space.

It is defined by geography, history, and long-term interaction rather than blood, ideology, or political authority.

Civilizations are not created by identity.
They are shaped by geography and time.

The Land–Sea System of Northeast Asia

Northeast Asia is not a collection of isolated states.
It is a single land–sea system formed through repeated interaction between continent and ocean.

For the purpose of this book, Northeast Asia refers consistently to five territories: Japan, the Korean Peninsula, China, Russia, and Mongolia (including Inner and Outer Mongolia).

From Eastern Siberia and Mongolia to Northern China, the Korean Peninsula, and the Japanese archipelago, a continuous pattern emerges:

- migration and settlement
- trade and exchange
- conflict and adaptation
- coexistence and balance

Where land and sea meet repeatedly, history accumulates.

This interaction predates modern borders and persists despite them.

A Large Economic Zone Already Exists

Regardless of political alignment, Northeast Asia already functions as:

- a large economic zone
- a shared logistics and energy system
- a common security environment

The population of this interconnected region exceeds 250 million.

Interdependence exists without a shared framework.

Integration without structure creates friction.
Structure without fairness creates resistance.

Patterns Older Than States

Nation-states are recent in historical terms.
The Pan Alta world is not.

Across recorded history, this region has been shaped by:

- steppe–forest interaction
- continental–maritime balance
- cycles of unification and fragmentation

Empires rose and collapsed.
Borders shifted.
Geography remained.

States change faster than geography.
Geography outlasts every state.

Why "Pan" Matters

"Pan" does not mean above nations.
It means across them.

Pan Alta does not deny sovereignty.
It recognizes that no sovereignty in this region exists in isolation.

Sovereignty survives not by denial of reality,
but by adaptation to it.

Why United Pan Alta

The future of Northeast Asia will be shaped by how effectively it balances Wealth and Freedom.

Wealth represents:

- economic capacity
- technological development
- material security

Freedom represents:

- sovereignty
- dignity
- cultural continuity
- choice

History demonstrates a consistent pattern.

Wealth without freedom produces domination.
Freedom without wealth produces vulnerability.

United Pan Alta is proposed not as an ideal, but as a structural solution.

Under current and foreseeable conditions, it is the most structurally efficient vision for:

- increasing shared wealth without centralization
- preserving freedom without isolation
- reducing conflict without uniformity

Efficiency in civilization is measured not by speed,
but by how much value is created with how little coercion.

In a region of continental scale and maritime complexity, fragmentation:

- duplicates cost
- magnifies insecurity
- wastes human potential

A fair, coordinated framework enables:

- economies of scale without loss of sovereignty
- cooperation without submission
- stability without stagnation

The most durable systems are those that expand wealth
while protecting freedom at the same time.

United Pan Alta does not promise outcomes.
It provides conditions.

It does not decide the future.
It expands the range of possible futures.

A good vision does not command history.
It prepares people to shape it.

Closing Anchor

United Pan Alta begins with recognition, not ambition.

Recognition of:

- shared space
- shared history
- shared future risk

The future of Northeast Asia will not be decided by power alone,
but by whether its people learn to prepare together.

PART II

Why Past Unifications Failed

Chapter 2 – Few Thousand Years of Failed Unification

The Repeating Pattern

Across a few thousand years, Northeast Asia has experienced repeated attempts at unification.

They differed in form:

- empires
- dynasties
- military alliances
- ideological blocs

They differed in scale and duration.

They shared one outcome.

Every forced unification in Northeast Asia eventually collapsed.

Unification by Power

Most historical attempts at unity relied on power first:

- military conquest
- centralized authority
- enforced hierarchy

These systems expanded quickly.
They stabilized briefly.
They declined inevitably.

Power can assemble space faster than it can hold it.

The problem was not ambition.
The problem was structure.

The Structural Flaw

Power-based unification failed because it treated control as unity.

Control requires:

- coercion
- compliance
- suppression of difference

Unity requires:

- legitimacy
- consent
- accommodation

Control produces order.
Only legitimacy produces unity.

Where legitimacy was absent, resistance accumulated—quietly or openly—until collapse followed.

Centralization and Its Limits

Centralized systems promised efficiency.
Over time, they produced fragility.

In a region defined by:

- vast geography
- diverse cultures
- continental and maritime interaction

centralization increased:

- administrative distance
- misallocation of resources
- systemic rigidity

The larger the space, the higher the cost of central control.

The Illusion of Permanence

Each dominant power believed its system to be final.

History disagreed.

No empire, dynasty, or hegemonic order proved permanent—not because of moral failure, but because of structural mismatch.

What ignores structural limits mistakes duration for permanence.

Temporary stability was repeatedly misread as historical resolution.

Fragmentation was not the cause of failure.

Fragmentation did not cause failure.
Fragmentation was the result.

When centralized systems lost legitimacy, regions reverted to:

- local autonomy
- regional balance
- defensive separation

Fragmentation follows collapse; it does not cause it.

The cycle repeated because its underlying logic remained unchanged.

Why Geography Always Reasserted Itself

Northeast Asia's geography resists permanent domination.

- Steppe and forest enable mobility
- Mountains and seas limit projection
- Maritime access decentralizes power

Geography does not negotiate.
It reasserts itself.

Attempts to override these realities produced short-lived orders and long-term instability.

The Missing Element

Across centuries, one element was consistently absent: fairness.

Not fairness as moral aspiration, but fairness as system design.

Systems failed because they:

- extracted more than they returned
- demanded loyalty without legitimacy
- centralized benefits while distributing costs

Unfair systems can expand.
They cannot endure.

Why This History Matters Now

This book does not revisit history to assign blame.

It does so to extract a structural lesson:

What failed repeatedly should not be repeated differently;
it should be replaced structurally.

Modern conditions do not erase historical limits.
They make them more consequential.

Closing Anchor

The failure of past unifications does not mean unity is impossible.

It means that forced unity is unsustainable.

Unity imposed by power collapses.
Unity prepared through fairness can endure.

United Pan Alta begins where history repeatedly failed—
not by rejecting it, but by learning from its structure.

— ✦ —

PART III

Structural Reality of Northeast Asia

Chapter 3 – The Structural Reality of Northeast Asia

A Region Without a Permanent Center

Northeast Asia has never sustained a permanent center of power.

At different times, influence shifted:

- across the continent
- toward the peninsula
- into the maritime sphere

No center endured.

In Northeast Asia, power circulates.
It does not settle.

This is not accidental.
It is structural.

Why No Hegemon Endures

Attempts at regional dominance consistently confronted the same limits:

- geographic scale
- cultural diversity
- land–sea asymmetry

Dominance required:

- expanding control
- increasing administrative reach
- suppressing regional autonomy

The cost rose faster than capacity.

The cost of control grows faster than the benefit of expansion.

Continental–Maritime Asymmetry

Northeast Asia is shaped by an inherent imbalance:

- continental depth on one side

- maritime openness on the other

Continental systems favor:

- scale
- centralization
- territorial continuity

Maritime systems favor:

- flexibility
- decentralization
- external connectivity

What stabilizes land destabilizes sea.
What empowers sea resists land.

No single structure can dominate both indefinitely.

Scale as a Structural Constraint

The region's size magnifies every decision.

As scale increases:

- coordination costs rise
- errors propagate faster
- rigidity becomes dangerous

Centralized systems initially appear efficient.
Over time, they lose adaptability.

Scale rewards coordination,
but punishes rigidity.

Diversity Is Not a Weakness

Northeast Asia contains:

- multiple languages
- distinct histories

- varied political systems

This diversity has often been treated as an obstacle to unity.

Structurally, it is a constraint—but also a stabilizer.

Uniformity accelerates control.
Diversity preserves resilience.

Systems that fail to accommodate difference accumulate stress.

Interdependence Without Architecture

Today, Northeast Asia is deeply interdependent.

Supply chains, energy flows, and security dynamics already cross borders.

Yet this interdependence lacks:

- shared rules
- stable expectations
- a fairness-based framework

Interdependence without architecture produces friction.

Without structure, shocks amplify rather than dissipate.

Why Balance Outperforms Dominance

History and structure point to the same conclusion.

In Northeast Asia:

- balance lasts longer than dominance
- coordination outperforms coercion
- legitimacy reduces cost

What is balanced requires less force to sustain.

Balance does not eliminate competition.
It constrains its destructiveness.

The Central Insight

The structural reality of Northeast Asia is not chaos.
It is misfit—between scale, geography, and governance models.

Attempts to impose unity failed because they ignored this reality.

Systems fail not from *bad intentions,*
but from structural mismatch.

Implication for the Future

Any viable vision for Northeast Asia must:

- respect scale
- accommodate diversity
- integrate land and sea
- minimize coercion

A future that contradicts structure will not arrive.

United Pan Alta does not attempt to override this reality.
It is designed to operate within it.

Structural Stress Points

Structural stress in Northeast Asia concentrates in three recurring areas:

- inland access to maritime trade
- energy dependency asymmetry
- power concentration around narrow corridors

When stress accumulates at these nodes, political tension follows.

Interior regions seek access.
Maritime regions seek leverage.
Gateways become pressure points.

United Pan Alta does not remove stress.
It redistributes and reduces it.

Stability is not achieved by eliminating difference.
It is achieved by preventing imbalance from compounding.

Closing Anchor

The question is no longer whether Northeast Asia will be interconnected.

It already is.

The question is whether this interconnection will remain unmanaged—or become fair and sustainable.

Structure determines outcomes long before intentions do.

A New Structural Layer

Geography shaped the first layer of Northeast Asian structure.

It determined where people settled, how trade moved, where empires expanded, and where they stopped.

Political borders shaped the second layer.

They formalized control, divided the land-sea continuum, and created the friction that still defines the region today.

A third layer is now forming.

Digital infrastructure is becoming as structurally determinative as geography once was.

Submarine cables carry the data flows that underpin regional trade, finance, and communication. Platform architectures determine which entrepreneurs can reach markets and which cannot. Data governance regimes are drawing new invisible borders — often more consequential in daily economic life than the physical ones they overlay.

The digital generation did not inherit a pre-digital world that later went online. They inherited a world where the digital layer was already present at birth — already shaping opportunity, access, and power before they were old enough to recognize it as a structure at all.

The most powerful structures are those that feel like nature.

How Digital Infrastructure Maps onto the Five Nodes

The five-node framework of the Structural Pentagon does not exist only in physical geography. It is being reproduced — and distorted — in digital space.

Node 1, the Mongolian Plateau, remains the most digitally underserved of the five nodes. Connectivity gaps translate directly into economic distance. A Mongolian entrepreneur faces higher effective barriers to global digital markets than counterparts in any of the four remaining nodes — not because of geography alone, but because digital infrastructure investment has followed existing power concentrations rather than structural need.

Node 2, Northeast China, possesses significant digital infrastructure but operates within a governance architecture that limits cross-border data flow. Its digital productivity is high internally. Its integration with the broader regional digital economy remains structurally constrained.

Node 3, Far East Russia, faces the compounded challenge of physical distance from both continental and maritime digital hubs. Its digital layer reflects the same isolation that its geography imposes — an underutilized node in both physical and digital terms.

Node 4, the Korean Peninsula, is among the most digitally advanced territories in the world by infrastructure density and connectivity speed. Yet its division means that one half of the peninsula's digital potential remains structurally severed — the most visible digital fracture in the region.

Node 5, the Japanese archipelago, possesses sophisticated digital architecture and deep integration with global technology systems. Its structural role in the digital layer mirrors its physical one: the interface between the Pan Alta interior and the global Pacific system.

Digital asymmetry reproduces physical asymmetry.
Where infrastructure is absent, distance returns.

The Risk of Digital Dominance

The same structural warning that applies to physical power applies to digital power.

When one node — or one external actor — concentrates control over the digital infrastructure that connects the region, the structural logic of dominance reasserts itself in a new form.

Platform monopolization is the digital equivalent of controlling a gateway port.

Data governance asymmetry is the digital equivalent of extractive trade terms.

Surveillance architecture is the digital equivalent of administrative occupation.

The form changes. The structural problem does not.

United Pan Alta cannot be built on digital infrastructure that reproduces the imbalances it seeks to correct. The Fair Wealth Protocol described in Chapter 11 addresses this directly. But its foundation must be recognized here: the digital layer of Northeast Asia is not neutral. It is already contested. And its architecture will shape the region's structural future as decisively as any railway or energy grid.

What the Digital Generation Inherits

The current and coming digital generation inherits a Northeast Asia that is physically divided but digitally porous.

They cross borders daily — in commerce, in culture, in communication — that their governments have not yet formally opened.

This is not a small thing.

A generation that already cooperates informally
is closer to structural alignment than any prior generation has been.

Their task is not to begin the work of connection. That work has already begun — through them, without their full awareness. Their task is to recognize what they are already doing, understand its structural significance, and choose to do it with intention rather than by accident.

Awareness transforms habit into architecture.

PART IV

Fairness, Wealth, and Freedom

Chapter 4 – Fairness as the Missing Architecture

Why Power Was Never Enough

History in Northeast Asia did not fail for lack of power.
It failed for lack of economic architecture that could endure.

Power assembled territory.
Power enforced order.
Power accelerated expansion.

What power did not sustain was economically sound growth over time.

Power can expand systems.
Only sound architecture can sustain prosperity.

Architecture Before Prosperity

Economic strength is not created by scale alone.
It is created by architecture that reduces friction.

Architecture determines:

- how wealth is generated
- how value circulates
- how incentives align
- how shocks are absorbed

Prosperity is not an outcome of ambition.
It is an outcome of structure.

Why Fairness Is Economically Structural

Fairness is often mistaken for a moral constraint.
In large systems, it is an economic efficiency mechanism.

Unfair systems:

- extract wealth unevenly
- raise transaction costs
- require enforcement

- discourage long-term investment

Unfair systems spend more energy controlling wealth than producing it.

Fairness lowers the cost of coordination and increases productive participation.

Fairness and Scale

As scale increases, unfairness becomes more expensive.

In small systems:

- inefficiency can be hidden
- imbalance can be delayed

In large regions like Northeast Asia:

- inefficiency compounds
- capital retreats
- instability becomes systemic

Scale rewards fairness more than force.

This is why fairness is not idealism—it is macroeconomic realism.

Fairness as the Foundation of Wealth

Sustained wealth requires:

- trust
- predictability
- voluntary participation

These cannot be imposed reliably.

Wealth grows fastest where participation is chosen,
not enforced.

Unfair systems may generate short-term extraction.
They undermine the conditions for continuous growth.

Freedom as an Economic Condition

Freedom in this book is not abstraction.
It is an operational requirement for economic strength.

Freedom enables:

- innovation
- mobility of talent
- adaptive decision-making
- long-term commitment

Without freedom, wealth becomes rigid.
Rigid wealth declines.

Freedom protects the system from stagnation.

The Balance Principle

Northeast Asia does not suffer from lack of capacity.
It suffers from imbalance.

- Wealth without freedom produces concentration and resistance
- Freedom without wealth produces fragility and dependence

Economic strength without freedom is unstable.
Freedom without economic strength is unsustainable.

United Pan Alta exists to resolve this imbalance structurally.

Why Fairness Was Missing

Past systems prioritized:

- power over productivity
- control over efficiency
- extraction over sustainability

Fairness was treated as secondary.

The result was repeated economic exhaustion.

What is treated as secondary eventually collapses the primary.

The Architectural Shift

United Pan Alta places:

- economic soundness first
- fairness as the operating architecture
- freedom as the stabilizing condition

Fairness is not added to growth.
It is built into growth.

This reduces coercion, lowers cost, and increases resilience.

Implication for United Pan Alta

United Pan Alta aims at a strong, economically sound Northeast Asia.

Not through centralization.
Not through uniformity.
Not through force.

But through:

- fair coordination
- protected freedom
- structurally efficient cooperation

The strongest economies are those
that require the least coercion to function.

Closing Anchor

The future strength of Northeast Asia will depend less on power than on how efficiently it converts cooperation into wealth—and how carefully it protects freedom in the process.

When fairness becomes economic architecture,
prosperity and freedom reinforce each other.

Chapter 5 – What United Pan Alta Is (and Is Not)

Why This Clarification Matters

Visions fail not only from opposition,
but from misunderstanding.

In regions shaped by history, power, and memory,
clarity is not optional.

*A vision that must be defended repeatedly
was never explained clearly enough.*

This chapter exists to remove ambiguity.

What United Pan Alta Is

United Pan Alta is:

- a long-term civilizational vision
- a fair, preparation-based framework
- a non-coercive path toward coordination
- a structural approach to economic strength
- a freedom-preserving model of cooperation

It is designed to:

- reduce systemic friction
- increase economic efficiency
- expand shared prosperity
- protect sovereign choice

*United Pan Alta coordinates interests.
It does not command behavior.*

What United Pan Alta Is Not

United Pan Alta is NOT:

- anti-China
- anti-Russia
- anti-Japan
- anti-Korea
- anti-Mongolia (Inner & Outer)
- anti-nation-state

It is NOT:

- a geopolitical bloc
- a military framework
- an ideological project
- a cultural hierarchy

Opposition defines enemies.
Architecture defines conditions.

What United Pan Alta Does Not Propose

United Pan Alta does not propose:

- political unification
- territorial change
- centralized authority
- compulsory institutions
- enforced timelines

What must be enforced
cannot be sustainable.

What United Pan Alta Respects

United Pan Alta respects:

- sovereignty
- cultural continuity

- voluntary participation
- diversity of systems
- historical experience

It assumes:

- interdependence already exists
- isolation is no longer cost-free
- coordination can occur without submission

Respect reduces the cost of cooperation.

Why United Pan Alta Is Economically Grounded

United Pan Alta is not an abstract ideal.

It responds to:

- overlapping supply chains
- shared energy risks
- demographic shifts
- rising coordination costs

Its purpose is to make:

- cooperation cheaper than conflict
- coordination more efficient than competition
- growth more stable than extraction

The strongest systems are those
that lower the cost of working together.

What Participation Means

Participation in United Pan Alta is:

- voluntary

- incremental
- reversible
- non-exclusive

No participant:

- surrenders sovereignty
- loses identity
- accepts permanent obligation

A vision survives when people can leave it.

What United Pan Alta Ultimately Seeks

United Pan Alta seeks:

- an economically sound and strong Northeast Asia
- increased shared wealth
- protected freedom
- reduced systemic risk

Not by force.
Not by uniformity.
Not by domination.

Strength built on fairness lasts longer than strength built on power.

Closing Anchor

United Pan Alta does not demand agreement.

It provides a framework within which disagreement becomes less costly and more productive.

Clarity is the first condition of trust.

This chapter closes the question of intent—
so the work of preparation can begin.

Part V

The Structural Pentagon: A Five-Node Architecture

Chapter 6 – The Five Pillars of the Structural Pentagon

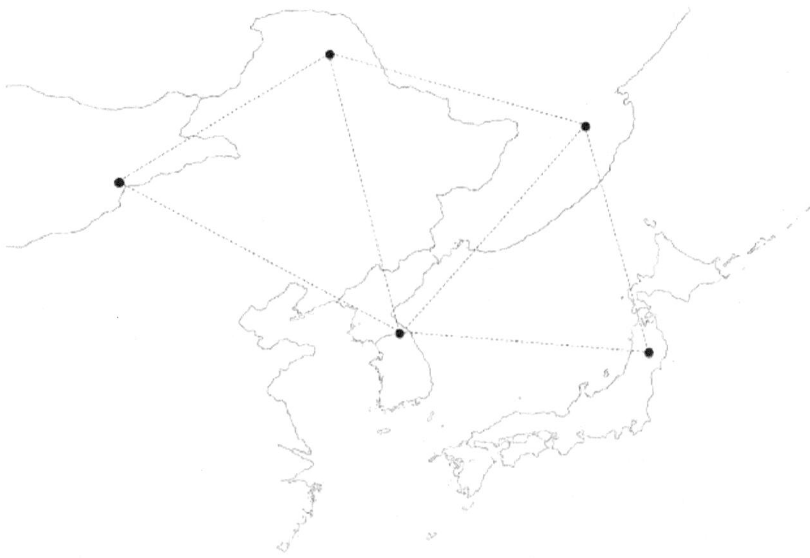

Figure 1. United Pan Alta – The Northeast Asia Land–Sea Continuum and Structural Pentagon Framework

The pentagon illustrates a structural relationship among five regional nodes within a continuous land–sea geography.

The Structural Pentagon Framework represents the geometric equilibrium of Northeast Asia. In the architectural design of this region, no single node is the "center." Instead, the center is the vacuum created by the balance of all five. For United Pan Alta to function, each of these five nodes must move away from the "dominance-based" models of the past and toward a "contribution-based" structural alignment.

Node 1: The Mongolian Plateau (The Continental Anchor) Mongolia represents the "deep interior" of the Pan Alta world. In previous centuries, this node was often isolated by distance or treated only as a resource buffer for neighboring powers. In the new architecture, Mongolia is the balance point. Its role is to provide the continental depth that prevents the region from becoming overly maritime-centric. By integrating Mongolia through high-speed terrestrial spines, we ensure the "Land" portion of the land-sea continuum is as dynamic as the coastal zones. The plateau is not the "back" of the region, but its foundational anchor. Without the stability of the Mongolian Plateau, the pentagon collapses inward.

Mongolia today stands at a structural inflection point.

Its vast reserves of coal, copper, and rare earth minerals — materials that the digital economy requires in increasing quantities — place it at the center of a global supply chain it has not yet fully entered on its own terms. The shift toward renewable energy across the region creates a new opportunity: the Mongolian Plateau receives among the highest solar irradiance and wind energy potential of any landmass in Northeast Asia.

This is not a distant possibility. It is a present structural asset that remains underleveraged because the infrastructure to carry its energy output to consuming nodes does not yet exist at regional scale.

For the digital generation, Mongolia represents something specific: a node whose structural importance is inverse to its current digital connectivity. The plateau that anchors the pentagon physically is the same plateau most underserved by the digital networks that will define the next century of regional wealth.

What the next generation builds toward Mongolia
will determine whether the pentagon holds or tilts.

The Structural Challenge: Overcoming the "Isolation of Distance." For Mongolia to act as the Anchor, the cost of transit across the plateau must be subsidized by the regional collective until the node reaches economic self-sufficiency.

Node 2: Northeast China (The Industrial Heartland) The provinces of Jilin, Heilongjiang, and Liaoning form the industrial and agricultural engine of the continental side. This node has the scale to drive regional wealth, but historically, its potential has been limited by a "bottleneck" geography—a lack of direct, integrated access to the sea. Within United Pan Alta, these provinces are no longer "inland" territories; they are structural partners with the coastal nodes. Their role is to provide the mass and energy of production that stabilizes the northern arc of the pentagon. Their integration removes the pressure of "continental enclosure" that often leads to regional friction.

The provinces of Jilin, Heilongjiang, and Liaoning carry a structural weight that is rarely acknowledged in proportion to its significance.

Together they represent one of the largest concentrations of industrial capacity, agricultural output, and engineering expertise in Northeast Asia. Yet for decades, their development trajectory has been shaped by internal priorities rather than regional integration — producing at scale for domestic consumption rather than functioning as a true node in a land-sea continuum.

The demographic challenge facing these provinces — aging populations, outward migration of younger workers toward coastal cities — is itself a structural signal. When a node cannot retain its productive generation, the pentagon weakens from within.

For the digital generation, Northeast China represents both a warning and an opportunity. A node of this scale, properly integrated into regional supply chains and digital commerce networks, becomes an engine for shared regional wealth. Underintegrated, it becomes a source of the continental enclosure pressure the Pan Alta framework is designed to release.

Scale without connection is weight without direction.

The Structural Challenge: Transitioning from an "Internal Engine" to a "Regional Partner." This requires a shift in mindset from provincial production to integrated regional supply chains that prioritize the health of the Tumen Gateway.

Node 3: Far East Russia (The Resource and Gateway Node) Far East Russia is the gateway to the Arctic and the vast northern frontier. It provides the "raw architecture" of the region—energy, minerals, and space. For too long, this node has been managed from a distant center that did not share its geographic fate. In the Pan Alta framework, it is a primary pillar. Its structural alignment involves transforming its port cities into shared regional gateways, ensuring that the northern wealth of the continent is distributed fairly across the land-sea continuum. This node ensures that Pan Alta is not just a southern trade network, but a holistic northern civilization.

The Structural Challenge: Managing the "Northern Pivot." As the Arctic opens, this node must ensure that the northern routes are managed as a common regional utility, preventing any single entity from monopolizing the gateway.

Far East Russia is undergoing a quiet but consequential transformation.

The opening of Arctic shipping routes — accelerated by changing climate conditions — is converting what was once a remote northern frontier into a potential transit corridor of global significance. The Northern Sea Route, connecting the Atlantic and Pacific through Arctic waters, passes through Far East Russia's sphere of geographic influence. What was peripheral is becoming central — not by political decision, but by physical reality.

This shift has not yet been matched by the regional institutional frameworks needed to manage it fairly. The risk is not that Far East Russia remains isolated. The risk is that its emerging gateway function is captured by a single external interest before a fair regional architecture exists to govern it.

For the digital generation, Far East Russia represents the most time-sensitive structural opportunity in the pentagon. The Arctic is opening now. The frameworks to govern it fairly must be prepared before the routes become indispensable — because once dependency is established, the terms of access become very difficult to renegotiate.

Preparation before dependency is strategy.
Preparation after dependency is negotiation from weakness.

Node 4: The Korean Peninsula (The Central Switchboard) As the geometric center of the pentagon, the Korean Peninsula is the physical bridge. It is the only node that is simultaneously deeply continental and deeply maritime. Its division in the 20th century was the primary "structural break" in Northeast Asia—a fractured bridge that forced the land and sea to remain separate. For the pentagon to hold, the peninsula must function as a frictionless conduit. It is the "switchboard" where the energy of the continent meets the trade of the ocean. Its stability is the litmus test for the health of the entire land-sea continuum.

The Structural Challenge: The "Neutrality Mandate." For the bridge to hold, the peninsula must remain structurally neutral. Any tilt toward one side of the pentagon at the expense of another causes the entire architecture to warp.

The Korean Peninsula occupies a position in the digital era that mirrors, and intensifies, its physical structural role.

South Korea is among the world's most digitally advanced societies — in infrastructure density, platform development, semiconductor manufacturing, and cultural digital exports. Its digital economy already crosses borders informally in ways its political situation does not permit formally. Korean entertainment, technology, and commerce reach into every other node of the pentagon, creating patterns of soft connectivity that political structures have not caught up with.

North Korea represents the sharpest digital fracture in the region — a node almost entirely severed from the digital layer that connects the rest of the pentagon. This severance is not only a humanitarian concern. It is a structural inefficiency of the highest order: a population and territory at the geographic center of the land-sea continuum, contributing nothing to and receiving nothing from the regional digital economy.

For the digital generation, the peninsula presents the most structurally consequential unresolved question in Northeast Asia. Not because of its political drama — but because its geographic position as the switchboard of the continuum means that the fracture running through it costs every other node, every day it persists.

A fractured bridge does not only stop those who wish to cross.
It raises the cost of travel for everyone on both sides.

Node 5: The Japanese Islands (The Maritime Interface) The Japanese archipelago forms the eastern boundary of the land-sea continuum. Its role is not to be a "barrier" or an "outpost," but to be the interface between Pan Alta and the global Pacific system. Japan's advanced technological and maritime architecture provides the sophisticated "outer shell" of the pentagon. Its structural responsibility is to ensure that the region's maritime trade routes are governed by fairness and transparency, preventing the "concentration of power" that leads to regional friction. Japan provides the "ventilation" through which the continental lungs of Pan Alta breathe.

The Structural Challenge: The "Integration Paradox." Japan must integrate its high-tech maritime architecture with the continental interior without falling into the old patterns of maritime dominance.

Japan's structural position in the digital era carries a particular responsibility.

As the most technologically sophisticated node in the pentagon, Japan possesses the architectural capacity to either accelerate or impede regional digital integration. Its semiconductor supply chains, robotics infrastructure, and deep integration with global financial and technology systems give it a structural leverage that no other node currently matches.

This leverage can be used in two ways.

It can be used to deepen connectivity across the pentagon — sharing technological architecture, reducing the digital asymmetry between coastal and interior nodes, and functioning as the interface through which the region connects to global systems on fair terms.

Or it can be used to reinforce the maritime advantage that history has repeatedly shown cannot be sustained indefinitely without generating continental resistance.

Japan has navigated this structural tension before — with varying results. The digital era presents the same choice in a new form. The technological sophistication that makes Japan the peninsula's most capable partner is the same sophistication that, if deployed extractively, recreates the structural imbalance the Pan Alta framework is designed to prevent.

For the digital generation in Japan, this is the inheritance: not guilt for history, but responsibility for architecture.

The most capable node carries the largest structural obligation.

"Stability is not found in the strength of one node, but in the tension and balance between all five."

The Structural Pentagon is not symbolic.
It is a cost-distribution model.

When one node dominates trade routes, energy supply, or transport corridors, the cost of adjustment rises for all others.

Dominance concentrates risk.
Balance distributes risk.

In a system of five nodes, equilibrium reduces systemic cost.
Imbalance increases the price of correction.

Structural balance is therefore not aesthetic.
It is economic.

— ✦ —

PART VI

Case Studies in Structural Alignment

Chapter 7 – The Tumen River Triad: A Gateway of Three Nodes

The Tumen River is the "architectural hinge" of the North. For Node 2 (Northeast China), Node 3 (Far East Russia), and Node 4 (Korea), this area has historically been a point of high structural friction. In the United Pan Alta model, we do not seek to move borders, but to dissolve the friction of the borders.

The triad alignment requires a "Three-Key System." No single node can unlock the potential of the northern gateway alone. When China's industrial mass, Russia's northern gateway ports, and Korea's peninsula-bridge logistics are aligned, the "land-locked" status of the interior vanishes. This is the first "proof of concept" for the land-sea continuum—showing that wealth is created not by owning the gate, but by keeping it open.

—✦—

Chapter 8 – The Energy Spine: From the Plateau to the Archipelago

The alignment between Node 1 (Mongolia) and Node 5 (Japan) represents the "Symmetry of Needs." The Mongolian Plateau is the battery of the region—rich in the minerals and renewable potential required for the new millennium. Japan is the processor—possessing the technological architecture to transform that potential into regional stability.

The structural bridge is the Peninsula (Node 4). When energy flows through this spine, it creates a mutual hostage to peace. Because the archipelago depends on the plateau for energy, and the plateau depends on the archipelago for market integration, conflict becomes a structural impossibility.

— ✦ —

Chapter 9 – The "Blue Ribbon" Maritime Alignment

This case study focuses on the maritime space between Node 5 (Japan) and Node 4 (Korea). Instead of competing for maritime dominance, these nodes align their port management and shipping lanes into a single "Blue Ribbon" corridor. By treating the sea between them as a shared internal lung rather than a contested border, they reduce the cost of logistics for the entire Pan Alta world.

"Case studies are not predictions; they are proofs of concept. They show that when geography is respected, the architecture of peace follows naturally."

Conclusion of Part VI: What the Case Studies Reveal

The three case studies do not exist independently of one another.

They are three expressions of the same underlying structural logic:

- The Tumen River Triad demonstrates the potential of a land gateway
- The Energy Spine demonstrates continental-maritime interdependence
- The Blue Ribbon Alignment demonstrates shared maritime corridors

When geography is respected, structure rewards cooperation.

When geography is ignored, structure punishes conflict.

These are not idealistic scenarios.

These are achievable alignments that show what becomes possible when structural realities are unleashed.

The first step is not conquest, but opening.

PART VII

The Infrastructure of Integration

Chapter 10 – Hard Alignments: The Physical Skeleton

For United Pan Alta to exist, the land-sea continuum must be braced by physical infrastructure that ignores traditional political barriers. These "Hard Alignments" are the skeleton upon which the body of the region hangs.

1. The Standardized Rail Gauge: The continental nodes (Mongolia, NE China, Far East Russia) and the peninsular bridge (Korea) must commit to a unified high-speed rail standard. This is not merely a transport project; it is the physical removal of "structural friction." When a container can move from Ulaanbaatar to Busan without stopping for a gauge change, the land and sea are officially integrated.

2. The Regional Energy Grid: We must move toward a "Synchronized Power Architecture." This allows renewable energy generated on the Mongolian Plateau to be utilized by the high-tech hubs of Japan and Korea in real-time. By sharing energy infrastructure, we create a system of mutual reliance where the health of one node is tied to the energy security of the others.

Infrastructure requires capital discipline.

Hard alignments must:

- distribute financing burden proportionally
- avoid debt dependency structures
- ensure revenue transparency across nodes

A shared railway that bankrupts one node is not alignment.
It is delayed instability.

An energy grid that concentrates pricing power recreates the imbalance it claims to solve.

United Pan Alta cannot be built on financial asymmetry.

Physical integration without economic fairness accelerates collapse.

Alignment must reduce long-term cost for all participants, not create short-term advantage for one.

Principles of the Phased Path

The phased path follows four principles:

- Voluntariness — no phase is compulsory
- Reversibility — participation can be adjusted
- Asymmetry — not all participants move at the same pace
- Fairness-first — legitimacy precedes scale

Phases exist to reduce risk, not to accelerate control.

Phase I – Intellectual and Cultural Preparation

The first phase is not institutional.
It is cognitive.

It focuses on:

- shared understanding
- conceptual alignment
- trust-building across societies

This includes:

- education and research exchange
- shared terminology and frameworks
- open, non-binding dialogue

Preparation begins when people can disagree using the same concepts.

No authority is created.
No obligation is imposed.

Phase II – Economic and Functional Coordination

Once understanding exists, coordination becomes economical.

This phase emphasizes:

- trade facilitation
- energy cooperation
- logistics efficiency
- risk-sharing mechanisms

Coordination remains:

- voluntary
- project-based
- non-exclusive

Economic cooperation succeeds when it lowers cost without narrowing choice.

Economic strength is pursued without centralization.

Phase III – Institutional Alignment Without Integration

Institutions may emerge—but only as enablers, not controllers.

This phase focuses on:

- standards alignment
- information transparency
- dispute management mechanisms

Institutions remain:

- light
- functional
- consent-based

Institutions should serve cooperation, not substitute for it.

Sovereignty remains intact.

Phase IV – Generational Continuity

The final phase is not completion.
It is continuity.

This phase ensures:

- knowledge transfer
- institutional memory
- adaptability to new conditions

A vision survives only when it outlives its authors.

Each generation reassesses:

- relevance
- structure
- participation

Why There Is No Timeline

United Pan Alta does not impose deadlines.

Timelines create pressure.
Pressure invites shortcuts.
Shortcuts undermine legitimacy.

What matures organically
requires less force to sustain.

Progress is measured by readiness, not speed.

Why Phases Can Overlap

Phases are not linear commands.
They may:

- overlap
- pause
- regress
- advance unevenly

Flexibility is not weakness.
It is structural intelligence.

The Role of States and Societies

States are not replaced.
Societies are not bypassed.

The phased path allows:

- governments to participate selectively
- institutions to cooperate functionally
- civil society to prepare culturally

Unity that excludes society
never survives government change.

Closing Anchor

United Pan Alta does not seek to arrive.
It seeks to remain viable.

A phased path protects freedom
while building strength.

Unity prepared patiently costs less
than unity enforced quickly.

— ✦ —

Chapter 11 – Soft Alignments: The Digital and Legal Interface

The physical skeleton requires a nervous system. These "Soft Alignments" ensure that the flow of wealth and information remains fair across all five nodes.

1. The Fair Wealth Protocol: A regional digital ledger that tracks the "Friction Coefficient" of trade. It ensures that the interior nodes are not being exploited by the maritime nodes through hidden logistical costs.

   The Fair Wealth Protocol does not regulate markets.

   It measures distortion.

   Transparency reduces suspicion.

   Measurement reduces manipulation.

   What is visible becomes harder to exploit.

   The purpose is not control.

   It is clarity.

   When friction is measured openly, adjustment becomes cooperative rather than confrontational.

   What the Digital Friction Coefficient Looks Like in Practice

   The Fair Wealth Protocol is not an abstract instrument.

   It measures something real — the structural disadvantage that interior nodes experience relative to maritime nodes in their ability to access, participate in, and benefit from regional and global economic systems.

   In the physical world, this disadvantage is visible: the cost of moving a container from Ulaanbaatar to a port is higher than moving the same container between coastal cities. The time is longer. The infrastructure is thinner. The options are fewer.

   In the digital world, the same disadvantage exists — but it is less visible, and therefore more easily ignored.

Consider two entrepreneurs of equal skill and ambition: one based in Ulaanbaatar, one based in Tokyo.

The entrepreneur in Tokyo accesses global digital payment systems with minimal friction. Her products reach international customers through platforms that recognize her currency, her legal framework, and her banking infrastructure. Her digital supply chain operates with low latency, high reliability, and broad market access.

The entrepreneur in Ulaanbaatar faces a different architecture. Payment platforms impose higher fees or are unavailable entirely. Logistics integrations are incomplete. Platform algorithms calibrated for high-volume markets deprioritize her listings. The digital infrastructure her business depends on was designed around nodes where density already exists — not around nodes where it needs to be built.

The digital economy does not begin from equality.
It begins from the infrastructure that already exists.

The Fair Wealth Protocol exists to make this disparity visible — measured, named, and tracked over time — so that adjustment becomes a matter of structural responsibility rather than individual complaint.

What is measured can be addressed.
What is invisible compounds silently.

Distributed Ledger Technology as the Backbone of Fairness

For the Fair Wealth Protocol to function, it requires an infrastructure that no single node controls.

This is not a minor requirement. It is the central structural challenge of any regional fairness mechanism: how do you create a measurement and accountability system that all five nodes trust, when no single node can be trusted by all others to administer it neutrally?

Distributed ledger technology — blockchain and its successors — offers a structural answer that prior eras did not have access to.

A distributed ledger does not reside in any single location. It is not administered by any single authority. Its records are transparent to all participants and alterable by none unilaterally. What is recorded on it is visible. What is visible is harder to manipulate.

For the Fair Wealth Protocol, this means:

Trade friction data — the time, cost, and barrier measurements that define the friction coefficient — can be recorded on a shared regional ledger that no single node populates alone and no single node can revise alone.

Energy flow data across the regional grid can be tracked with the same transparency — ensuring that the terms of exchange between energy-producing and energy-consuming nodes remain visible and therefore contestable if they drift toward extraction.

Infrastructure financing contributions and returns can be recorded in a form that makes hidden dependency structures visible before they become permanent.

Transparency does not guarantee fairness.
But opacity guarantees the possibility of unfairness.

The digital generation is the first in Northeast Asian history that possesses the technological literacy to build, operate, and maintain this kind of infrastructure. They do not need to wait for governments to design it. They can begin building the conceptual and technical architecture now — as researchers, as engineers, as entrepreneurs, as designers — so that when political conditions allow its formal adoption, the tools are already ready.

Preparation precedes possibility.
Tools prepared in advance cost less than tools built under pressure.

Transparency as the Modern Open Trade Route

For most of Northeast Asian history, the structural advantage of maritime nodes over interior nodes derived from a simple geographic reality: those who controlled the ports controlled the terms of trade.

Information asymmetry reinforced this advantage. The merchant at the port knew prices, demand, and route conditions that the producer in the interior did not. This knowledge gap was not incidental. It was structural — and it was exploited structurally.

The digital era has the technical capacity to eliminate this asymmetry entirely.

When prices are visible across all nodes simultaneously, the information advantage of gateway controllers disappears. When logistics costs are tracked transparently, hidden extraction becomes visible. When trade friction is measured and published, the political cost of maintaining unfair terms rises.

Open information is the digital equivalent of open trade routes.
Both reduce the structural power of those who benefit from controlling access.

This is why the Fair Wealth Protocol is not merely an accounting tool. It is a structural equalizer — one that uses the transparency capabilities of digital systems to correct the information asymmetries that have historically kept interior nodes at a structural disadvantage.

United Pan Alta does not ask interior nodes to trust maritime nodes.

It asks all nodes to trust a system that none of them controls alone.

Trust in a fair system
is more durable than trust in a powerful partner.

2. The Structural Neutrality Accord: A legal framework specifically for Node 4 (the Korean Peninsula) and Node 3 (Far East Russia gateways). These areas must be designated as "Structural Commons"—zones where the regional interest of balance overrides the local interest of dominance.

History Does Not Repeat, Conditions Do

History does not repeat itself mechanically.

What repeats are conditions.

Throughout its long history, Northeast Asia lacked the conditions necessary for sustainable coordination.

Those conditions are now changing.

Possibility emerges when conditions align,
not when intentions intensify.

The End of Expansion as a Solution

For most of history, growth came from expansion:

- territory
- population
- extraction

Expansion resolved scarcity temporarily.

It intensified conflict permanently.

What once solved scarcity
now multiplies risk.

In the current millennium, expansion has reached its limits.

Technology Changes Coordination Costs

The most significant shift is not power.
It is coordination cost.

Digital systems reduce:

- information asymmetry
- transaction cost
- distance penalties

When coordination becomes cheap,

cooperation becomes rational.

This change did not exist in earlier eras.

Economic Interdependence Is Now Structural

Interdependence is no longer optional.

Supply chains, energy systems, and financial flows now bind the region regardless of political alignment.

Decoupling increases cost
faster than it restores autonomy.

This makes unmanaged interdependence a liability.

Wealth Is Now Knowledge-Intensive

Modern wealth is:

- intangible
- networked
- innovation-driven

It depends on:

- openness
- trust
- freedom of movement

Knowledge economies collapse under coercion.

This fundamentally alters the relationship between power and prosperity.

Demography Alters Incentives

Population trends now favor:

- stability over conquest
- productivity over expansion
- cooperation over dominance

When growth slows, waste becomes unaffordable.

Demographic reality rewards efficiency.

Energy and Environment Constrain Power

Energy systems are shifting from:

- concentrated extraction
- toward distributed, diversified sources

Environmental limits now impose real costs.

What damages the system
eventually damages the strongest actor first.

Power that ignores constraints becomes expensive.

Freedom as a Competitive Advantage

In the current millennium, freedom is not a luxury.

It is a competitive advantage.

Freedom enables:

- innovation
- adaptability
- resilience

Systems that restrict choice
restrict their own future.

This changes the calculus of control.

Why This Moment Matters

The conditions that once prevented fair coordination are weakening.

The conditions that reward it are strengthening.

What was impossible yesterday
becomes inefficient to resist today.

United Pan Alta does not rely on optimism.
It relies on structural alignment.

Closing Anchor

This book is written now because now is different.

Not because conflict has ended,
but because its cost has risen.

When cooperation becomes cheaper than conflict,
preparation becomes responsibility.

Part VIII

Preparation for the Next Generation

Chapter 12 – Generational Responsibility

A Message Across Time

This book is written across generations.

It speaks to those living now,
and to those who will live with the consequences.

The future is not inherited equally.
Preparation determines who carries the burden.

To the Current Generation

The responsibility of the current generation is not to decide the future.

It is to prepare the conditions under which better decisions become possible.

Preparation means:

- understanding structure
- reducing avoidable risk
- resisting false urgency

Those who act without preparation
often force the next generation to repair.

This book does not ask the current generation to unify Northeast Asia.
It asks them not to make unity impossible.

To the Next Generation

The next generation will decide:

- whether cooperation deepens or fractures
- whether wealth expands or concentrates
- whether freedom survives or contracts

Their decisions will be constrained—or enabled—by what is prepared now.

Choice expands when preparation precedes power.

This book does not instruct the next generation what to choose.
It seeks to preserve their freedom to choose.

Why This Is a Shared Responsibility

No generation owns history.

Each generation:

- inherits conditions
- alters trajectories
- passes consequences

What is unprepared today becomes unavoidable tomorrow.

United Pan Alta exists to lengthen time horizons,
so decisions are made with awareness rather than urgency.

The Role of Vision

A vision is not a promise.
It is not a guarantee.
It is not a command.

A vision is a reference point.

A good vision does not remove uncertainty. It reduces blindness.

United Pan Alta is offered as such a reference.

The Final Measure

The success of United Pan Alta will not be measured by:

- treaties signed
- institutions created
- declarations made

It will be measured by:

- reduced cost of cooperation
- increased shared prosperity

- preserved freedom of choice

What endures quietly matters more than what announces itself loudly.

Closing Anchor

This book ends where responsibility begins.

The future of Northeast Asia will be shaped
not by those who demanded unity,
but by those who prepared for it.

Chapter 13 – The Digital Generation as Structural Agent

You Are Already Doing It

There is a question this book has not yet asked directly.

Not whether the digital generation *can* become structural agents of the Pan Alta vision.

But whether they realize they *already are.*

Every day, without formal agreement or institutional mandate, the current and coming digital generation crosses the borders that divided their grandparents' world. They purchase from sellers in nodes they could not locate on a map. They consume content produced in languages they do not speak, translated by systems they did not build, delivered through infrastructure they did not design. They collaborate on platforms that do not recognize national boundaries as relevant categories.

This is not politics. It is not ideology. It is not even intention.

It is structural behavior — and it is already reshaping the region.

The question is not whether this generation will participate in the Pan Alta continuum. They already do. The question is whether they will do so with awareness — as architects — or without it, as raw material for systems designed by others.

Participation without awareness is not agency.
It is consumption.

What Makes This Generation Structurally Different

Every prior generation in Northeast Asia faced the same foundational constraint: the cost of crossing borders was high.

High in money. High in time. High in political risk. High in cultural distance.

These costs were not accidents. They were structures — built, maintained, and enforced by systems that benefited from the friction they created.

The digital generation is the first in the history of this region for whom the baseline cost of cross-border interaction has dropped to near zero.

A message costs nothing. A transaction costs a small fee. A collaboration costs time and skill — but not permission.

When the cost of cooperation falls,
the architecture of separation becomes a choice rather than a necessity.

This is the structural shift that makes the current moment different from every prior moment in Northeast Asian history. Not the goodwill of leaders. Not the signing of treaties. Not the resolution of territorial disputes.

The cost structure has changed.

And the generation that inhabits this new cost structure — that has never known a world where geographic distance meant informational distance — is the first generation for whom the Pan Alta vision is not idealism.

It is simply a description of what already exists,
waiting to be recognized.

The Habits That Are Already Architecture

The digital generation does not need to be persuaded that cross-border cooperation is possible.

They practice it daily — often without naming it.

When a developer in Busan contributes to an open-source project maintained by a team in Tokyo and used by engineers in Ulaanbaatar, that is a functioning node relationship operating without institutional permission.

When a small business owner in Shenyang sells through a platform that delivers to customers in Seoul, that is the land-sea continuum in commercial operation.

When a student in Vladivostok uses educational content produced in Seoul to prepare for an examination, that is the transfer of knowledge across a node boundary that political history has kept formally closed.

These are not metaphors.

They are the early infrastructure of a regional architecture that is being built from below, by behavior, before it is ever ratified from above, by agreement.

What is built from below is harder to dismantle
than what is imposed from above.

The digital generation is not waiting for permission to integrate. They have already begun. The Pan Alta framework does not ask them to start. It asks them to recognize what they have started — and to continue with intention.

The Specific Responsibility of This Generation

Recognition alone is not enough.

The digital generation carries a structural responsibility that prior generations did not face in the same form: the architecture of their world is still being built, and they are among its builders — whether they acknowledge it or not.

The platforms they use are not neutral. The data systems they populate are not passive. The digital infrastructure they inhabit every day is making choices — about who has access, who bears cost, who accumulates power — and those choices are becoming harder to reverse with every passing year.

Infrastructure that seems invisible
is simply infrastructure that has already won.

The responsibility of the digital generation is therefore specific:

To ask, of every digital system they inhabit: *does this distribute access fairly across the five nodes, or does it concentrate advantage in one?*

To resist, in their own professional and creative work: *the temptation to optimize for speed at the cost of structural fairness.*

To prepare, in their thinking and their networks: *the conceptual ground on which fair digital architecture can be built before unfair architecture becomes irreversible.*

This is not a political program.

It is structural maintenance — the same discipline that any architect applies to any system they wish to remain standing.

Balance does not maintain itself.
It requires those who recognize its value
to choose it, repeatedly, in small decisions.

Becoming Architects of Balance

The existing Chapter 14 of this book calls on the reader to become an Architect of Balance — to guard against power concentration in any single node and to strengthen the others when imbalance appears.

That call was written for the physical and political architecture of the region.

It applies equally — perhaps more urgently — to the digital architecture now being built on top of it.

The digital generation has tools their predecessors did not. They can build platforms that distribute rather than concentrate. They can design systems that reduce the friction coefficient for the interior nodes rather than amplifying it. They can create content, frameworks, and networks that carry the Pan Alta conceptual vocabulary across the region without requiring translation by governments or institutions.

The most durable architecture is built
by those who understand both the structure and the stakes.

You are the first generation for whom both are accessible.

The structure is described in this book.

The stakes are the world you are already living in.

What you build with that knowledge
is the only question that remains open.

— ✦ —

Chapter 14 – The Architecture of Balance

You are the first generation to inherit a Northeast Asia that is technically capable of total integration. Previous generations were limited by the lack of physical infrastructure; you are limited only by the architecture of your thinking.

The "Pan Alta" mind does not ask "Who owns this land?" but "How does this land serve the continuum?" Your responsibility is to guard against the "Power Concentration" that destroyed the stability of your ancestors. If you see one node becoming too dominant, it is your duty to strengthen the other four. This is not politics—it is the maintenance of a durable structure.

You must become Architects of Balance.

TECHNICAL APPENDIX
The Structural Metrics of Pan Alta

For the vision of United Pan Alta to remain grounded in reality, the current and next generations must have objective benchmarks to measure progress. These metrics are the "vitals" of the land-sea continuum:

1. The friction coefficient: measuring the time and cost it takes for a citizen of the interior (Mongolia) to reach the global ocean compared to a coastal citizen. Success is defined by the reduction of this gap.

2. The generational literacy rate: measuring how many young people in all five nodes can identify the "structural pentagon" and the "land-sea continuum" as their primary geographic reality.

3. Corridor Redundancy Index
   Measuring the number of viable alternative routes between nodes.
   Stability increases when no single corridor becomes indispensable.

4. Energy Interdependence Ratio
   Measuring the percentage of regional energy crossing at least one additional node before final consumption.
   Interdependence reduces unilateral leverage.

5. Governance Friction Index
   Measuring the average time required to resolve cross-border disputes affecting trade, infrastructure, or transit.
   Lower resolution time indicates higher structural maturity.

— ✦ —

Metrics do not enforce behavior.
They reveal imbalance before it escalates.

Regional Snapshot
Where Each Node Stands Today

A Structural Reading of the Present

This section does not offer political commentary.

It offers a structural reading — a brief assessment of where each of the five nodes currently stands in relation to the United Pan Alta framework, based on observable conditions rather than political judgment.

The purpose is practical.

The digital generation inherits not an abstract vision but a concrete regional reality. Understanding where each node currently stands — its structural strengths, its structural gaps, and its most immediate challenges — is the first step toward recognizing what preparation is actually required.

A map that only shows the destination
is less useful than one that also marks the current position.

These snapshots are intentionally concise. They are starting points for observation, not conclusions. Each generation must update them as conditions change.

Node 1: Mongolia — The Underleveraged Anchor

Mongolia's structural position within the pentagon is inverse to its current integration.

Its geographic centrality — as the continental anchor that prevents the land-sea continuum from becoming purely maritime-centric — is matched by a structural gap in the infrastructure needed to activate that centrality. Rail connectivity remains limited. Digital infrastructure lags significantly behind the four remaining nodes. Energy export capacity, despite vast renewable potential, has not yet been developed at regional scale.

What Mongolia possesses in abundance is structural asset value that has not yet been converted into structural participation.

Its rare earth mineral reserves are increasingly critical to the digital economy that the rest of the region depends on. Its renewable energy potential — solar and wind — positions it as the natural battery of the pentagon in the coming energy transition. Its land area provides the spatial foundation for transit corridors that no other node can offer. The structural challenge is not capacity. It is connectivity.

Mongolia today is a node of high potential and low activation. The generation that builds the infrastructure to close this gap — in rail, in energy transmission, in digital connectivity — will have done more to stabilize the pentagon than any political agreement could achieve.

The anchor that cannot be reached
provides no stability.

Node 2: Northeast China — The Restless Heartland

Northeast China — the provinces of Jilin, Heilongjiang, and Liaoning — is the most structurally paradoxical node in the pentagon.

It possesses industrial scale, agricultural depth, and engineering capacity that no other continental node can match. Yet its trajectory over the past three decades has been one of relative economic decline within China's broader development story — as investment, talent, and opportunity have migrated toward coastal provinces better positioned for maritime trade.

This internal migration pattern is itself a structural signal. When a node's most productive generation leaves, the node is communicating something about the adequacy of its current integration into the broader system.

Northeast China is not failing — it is misaligned. Its industrial strengths are calibrated for a closed continental economy, not an open regional one.

The Tumen River corridor represents the most immediate structural opportunity: direct access to maritime trade through a gateway that three nodes share. If that corridor activates, Northeast China's continental enclosure pressure releases. If it remains underutilized, the provinces continue their slow structural drift.

For the digital generation, Northeast China is the node where structural intervention has the highest potential return — and the highest cost of continued inaction.

A heartland that cannot reach the sea
pumps wealth inward, not outward.

Node 3: Far East Russia — The Opening Frontier

Far East Russia is the node undergoing the most consequential structural transformation in the current period.

The Arctic is opening. This is not a future possibility — it is a present reality, accelerating with each passing year. The Northern Sea Route is already operational for an increasing portion of the year, converting what was once a geographic extreme into a potential transit corridor connecting the Atlantic and Pacific at significantly reduced distances compared to existing southern routes.

Far East Russia sits at the center of this transformation. Its port cities — Vladivostok, Nakhodka, Magadan — are positioned to become regional gateways of global significance if the institutional frameworks to govern them fairly can be built before single-actor capture occurs.

The structural risk is timing. Infrastructure and dependency are developing faster than the regional frameworks needed to ensure that the benefits of the Arctic opening are distributed across all five nodes rather than concentrated in one external relationship.

The digital generation faces a specific challenge here: Far East Russia is the node least integrated into the digital networks that connect the other four. Its structural transformation is occurring in the physical layer — in shipping lanes and energy pipelines — while its digital layer remains underdeveloped. Building digital connectivity alongside physical infrastructure, rather than after it, is the preparation this node most urgently requires.

A gateway governed by one
is not a gateway.
It is a toll.

Node 4: The Korean Peninsula — The Fractured Switchboard

The Korean Peninsula is simultaneously the most digitally advanced and the most structurally fractured node in the pentagon.

South Korea's digital economy is among the most sophisticated in the world. Its semiconductor industry, platform development capacity, cultural digital exports, and infrastructure density place it at the technological frontier of the region. It already functions as a de facto interface node — connecting continental and maritime systems through commerce, culture, and technology in ways that its formal political situation does not fully reflect.

North Korea represents the sharpest structural absence in the entire framework. A territory and population at the geographic center of the land-sea continuum, contributing nothing to and receiving nothing from the regional digital economy, is not merely a humanitarian concern. It is a structural inefficiency that costs every other node every day it persists. The switchboard at the center of the pentagon is operating at half capacity — and the half that is missing is precisely the half that would connect the continental interior to the maritime exterior most directly.

The peninsula's structural neutrality — its capacity to function as a frictionless conduit rather than a tilted bridge — remains the single most consequential unresolved structural question in Northeast Asia.

For the digital generation, the peninsula presents both the region's greatest structural bottleneck and its greatest structural opportunity. What changes here changes the entire architecture.

When the switchboard is fractured,
every connection in the system
carries higher cost.

Node 5: Japan — The Sophisticated Interface

Japan is the most structurally mature node in the pentagon — and the one facing the most consequential internal structural challenge.

Its technological sophistication, maritime architecture, financial depth, and global integration give it capabilities that no other node currently possesses. As the interface between the Pan Alta interior and the global Pacific system, Japan's structural role is irreplaceable in the near to medium term. No other node can perform the ventilation function that Japan provides — connecting the continental mass to global trade flows with the efficiency and reliability that sophisticated maritime infrastructure enables.

The internal challenge is demographic. Japan's population is declining and aging at a rate that no other developed economy has yet navigated successfully. This demographic reality is not merely a domestic concern — it is a structural signal about the node's long-term capacity to maintain its current level of sophistication and engagement. A node that cannot sustain its productive population faces the same structural risk as any other: the pentagon weakens from within.

Japan's structural responsibility in the current period is therefore dual. To maintain and deepen its interface function for as long as its demographic capacity allows. And to invest in the regional digital architecture that will allow its technological contributions to outlast the demographic constraints that will eventually limit its physical capacity.

The most sophisticated node
carries the largest responsibility
to ensure its sophistication serves the whole.

Reading the Snapshot as a System

Taken together, these five snapshots reveal a region that is structurally ready for preparation — but not yet ready for integration.

Mongolia's potential is underleveraged. Northeast China is misaligned. Far East Russia is transforming faster than its governance frameworks can manage. The Korean Peninsula is fractured at its structural center. Japan is sophisticated but demographically constrained.

None of these conditions are permanent. All of them are addressable — not by political will alone, but by the sustained preparation that this book describes.

The snapshot today is not the forecast for tomorrow.
It is the starting point from which preparation begins.

The digital generation that reads these conditions clearly — and prepares accordingly — is the generation that will determine whether the pentagon stabilizes or continues to drift.

— ✦ —

CONDITIONS CHECKLIST
A Reference for the Current and Next Generation

This checklist is not a plan.

It is a readiness test.

United Pan Alta becomes viable only when most of these conditions are present.

Economic Conditions

- Cooperation reduces cost more than conflict
- Shared projects create net value for all participants
- Wealth creation is sustained, not extractive
- Economic gains do not require centralization

Why these conditions matter:

Economic conditions are the foundation upon which everything else rests. When cooperation genuinely costs less than conflict — not in theory, but in measurable transaction terms — participants choose coordination without being asked. When shared projects create net value for all nodes, the incentive to defect from the framework disappears. The critical word here is "sustained." Extractive wealth creation may produce short-term gains for one node while quietly depleting the conditions that make the next cycle of growth possible. A regional framework built on extraction is borrowing against its own future.

What absence looks like:

When economic conditions are absent, participants engage in the framework selectively — taking when advantageous, withdrawing when not. The result is not collapse but erosion: slow, uneven, and difficult to reverse once it has accumulated.

Freedom Conditions

- Participation is voluntary and reversible

- Sovereignty remains intact
- Cultural continuity is protected
- Innovation is not constrained by coercion

Why these conditions matter:

Freedom conditions are not idealistic additions to an otherwise economic framework. They are structural requirements. Voluntary and reversible participation ensures that the framework remains legitimate over time — because what cannot be exited cannot be trusted. Sovereignty intact means that no node is required to subordinate its fundamental decision-making capacity to the framework's momentum. Cultural continuity protected means that integration does not become a slow form of erasure. Innovation unconstrained by coercion means that the region's capacity to adapt — its most important long-term asset — remains alive.

What absence looks like:

When freedom conditions are absent, participation becomes performance. Nodes remain formally inside the framework while withdrawing genuine engagement. Legitimacy erodes faster than institutions can compensate for it.

Structural Conditions

- Coordination costs are lower than enforcement costs
- Fairness is embedded in system design
- Disagreement does not escalate automatically
- Exit remains possible without punishment

Why these conditions matter:

Structural conditions are the operating logic of the framework itself. When coordination costs fall below enforcement costs, fairness becomes economically rational rather than morally aspirational — which is the only basis on which it can be sustained at regional scale. When fairness is embedded in system design rather than added as a policy layer, it does not depend on the goodwill of any single actor to function. Disagreement that does not automatically escalate is the sign of a mature system — one that has built friction-management into its architecture rather than relying on the absence of friction. Exit without punishment is perhaps the most important structural condition of all: a framework that punishes departure is a framework that has replaced legitimacy with coercion.

What absence looks like:

When structural conditions are absent, the framework functions only under favorable circumstances. The first serious disagreement between nodes reveals the absence of the mechanisms needed to contain it — and what was presented as coordination reveals itself as fragile dependency.

Institutional Conditions

- Institutions serve function, not authority
- Rules are predictable and transparent
- Legitimacy precedes enforcement
- Adaptability is preserved

Why these conditions matter:

Institutions are the memory of a framework. They carry agreements forward across changes in leadership, shifts in political conditions, and the natural turnover of generations. But institutions that serve authority rather than function become obstacles to the cooperation they were created to enable. Rules that are predictable and transparent lower the cost of participation for every node — because uncertainty is itself a form of friction. Legitimacy that precedes enforcement means that rules are followed because they are seen as fair, not because violation carries a penalty. Adaptability preserved means that the framework can evolve with changing conditions rather than hardening into a structure that no longer fits the reality it governs.

What absence looks like:

When institutional conditions are absent, the framework loses continuity across generations. What one generation built with shared understanding, the next inherits as an obligation without context — and obligations without context are the first things discarded when conditions change.

Generational Conditions

- Knowledge is transferred across generations
- Long-term risks are acknowledged
- Short-term gains do not mortgage the future
- Preparation is valued over urgency

Why these conditions matter:

Generational conditions are the longest-horizon requirements in this checklist — and therefore the most frequently neglected. Knowledge transferred across generations means that the conceptual work of preparation does not need to be repeated from the beginning each time a new cohort inherits responsibility. Long-term risks acknowledged means that the framework is stress-tested against scenarios that have not yet occurred, not only optimized for conditions that currently exist. Short-term gains that do not mortgage the future means that the framework resists the permanent temptation to convert long-term structural assets into immediate political returns. Preparation valued over urgency is the single condition that most directly reflects the philosophy of this entire book.

What absence looks like:

When generational conditions are absent, the framework becomes generationally shallow — powerful in the hands of those who built it, irrelevant to those who inherited it without understanding why it was built. A vision that cannot be passed on is a vision that ends with its authors.

Final Test

If these conditions are absent,
do not advance unity.

If these conditions are present,
unity may emerge naturally.

Conditions determine outcomes
long before decisions are made.

A Note for the Digital Generation on Using This Checklist:

This checklist is not a scoring system.

It is a structural mirror.

The digital generation is the first in Northeast Asian history with the tools to monitor these conditions in near real-time — through data, through platform transparency, through the distributed networks they already inhabit. They do not need to wait for governments to assess readiness. They can observe, measure, and discuss these conditions themselves — in the same digital spaces where they already exchange everything else.

The checklist is most powerful when it becomes a shared language —
used across nodes, across borders, and across generations
to ask the same questions at the same time.

When a generation can agree on what readiness looks like, it becomes harder for those in power to claim readiness prematurely — or to deny it indefinitely.

Conditions do not announce themselves.
They must be read.

Book Closure

United Pan Alta does not close a debate.
It opens a timeframe.

Preparation is the quiet work
that makes history less violent.

— ✦ —

Questions for Future Generations

A Note on These Questions

This book has offered definitions, frameworks, and structural analysis.

It closes its preparatory work with something different.

Questions.

Not rhetorical questions — questions that already contain their answers. But genuine open questions: ones that this book cannot answer, that no single generation can answer, and that will require sustained collective intelligence across decades to even approach.

They are offered here not as problems to be solved but as responsibilities to be carried.

A generation that knows which questions matter
is already better prepared than one that does not.

These questions belong to the current and coming digital generation — not because they are the only ones who will face them, but because they are the first ones for whom the tools to begin answering them actually exist.

On Fairness

When does coordination become coercion?

Every framework that begins as voluntary has the potential to become, over time, a structure that is too costly to leave. At what point does the interdependence that United Pan Alta seeks to build cross the line from mutual benefit into mutual dependency — and how will the generation that inherits the framework recognize that line before it is crossed?

What is the minimum architecture of fairness
that a system of this scale requires to remain legitimate?

Is fairness between nodes of vastly different size and power structurally achievable — or does scale asymmetry inevitably produce extraction, regardless of intention?

On Wealth

What kind of wealth is the region actually building toward?

The digital economy creates wealth that is intangible, mobile, and unevenly distributed by design. Platform economies concentrate returns at the center and distribute costs to the periphery — reproducing, in digital form, the same structural asymmetry that the Pan Alta framework seeks to correct in physical form.

Can a regional framework built on fairness
coexist with a digital economy built on concentration?
And if not, which one changes?

At what point does shared infrastructure become shared dependency — and how does a region of sovereign states distinguish between the two before it is too late to choose differently?

On Freedom

How will the next generation know when coordination has gone too far?

United Pan Alta is designed to expand freedom by reducing the structural vulnerability that comes from isolation. But every coordination mechanism also creates new constraints — on what participants can do unilaterally, on how quickly they can change direction, on what exit actually costs in practice.

What are the early warning signs that a framework
built to protect freedom
has begun to quietly erode it?

And who is responsible for reading those signs — governments, institutions, or the ordinary people whose daily choices constitute the framework's actual operating reality?

On Power

Can a region with the structural history of Northeast Asia sustain balance without a dominant power to enforce it?

Every historical period of relative stability in the region has involved either a dominant power imposing order or an external threat creating temporary alignment. United Pan Alta proposes a third possibility: balance maintained through fairness rather than dominance. But this has no clear historical precedent in the region at this scale.

What makes the current moment genuinely different
from every prior moment when the same hope existed —
and how will the next generation know if that difference is real
or another temporary condition mistaken for permanence?

On Technology

Who governs the digital infrastructure of the region — and by what legitimacy?

The platforms, data systems, and AI architectures that will increasingly shape economic life across all five nodes are being built now, largely by actors whose interests are not defined by regional balance. The generation that inherits these systems will inherit not only their capabilities but their embedded assumptions about who deserves access, who bears cost, and who accumulates power.

Is it possible to retrofit fairness into digital infrastructure
after it has already been built around different values?
Or does fair digital architecture require
being present at the moment of construction?

And if the latter — is that moment already passing?

On Generations

How does a vision survive the generation that created it?

United Pan Alta was written by one generation for the next. But every vision that outlives its authors is also interpreted, adapted, and sometimes distorted by those who inherit it. The fixed definitions in this book are an attempt to anchor meaning across that transition — but definitions cannot enforce themselves.

What does the next generation owe to the generation
that prepared the conceptual ground they are standing on?
And what does it owe to the generation after itself —
the one that cannot yet speak on its own behalf?

Is preparation a gift — or an obligation? And if it is an obligation, to whom is it owed, and how is that debt repaid?

On Unity

What would genuine unity in Northeast Asia actually feel like — and would anyone recognize it if it arrived?

United Pan Alta deliberately avoids defining unity as an endpoint. It treats unity as an emergent condition — something that appears when the structural conditions for it are present, not something that is declared or achieved through a singular act.

But emergence without recognition is invisible.
How will the current and coming generations know
when the region has moved from preparation toward something more?
And how will they avoid mistaking temporary alignment
for the durable structure they were preparing for?

A Final Note on These Questions

These questions are not obstacles.

They are the work.

A generation that dismisses them as unanswerable has misunderstood what preparation means. A generation that treats them as already answered has misunderstood what this book is for.

Questions of this kind are not solved.
They are carried — carefully, across time,
by those who understand why they matter.

This book does not end with answers.

It ends with the questions worth asking.

What comes next belongs to those
who are willing to ask them.

— ✦ —

What Could Cause Failure

United Pan Alta is not immune to collapse.

It could fail if:

- one node seeks renewed dominance
- external powers exploit structural imbalance
- debt structures create hidden dependency
- demographic decline accelerates fragmentation
- technology centralizes power instead of distributing it

Architecture fails when maintenance stops.

No design survives without vigilance.

Balance is not self-executing.
Fairness is not self-sustaining.

The cost of imbalance rises slowly—
until correction becomes disruptive.

United Pan Alta requires continuous recalibration.

Structural durability depends less on ambition
than on disciplined restraint.

The Digital Failure Scenario

The physical and political failure scenarios described above are familiar to history.

A new category of failure has no historical precedent — because the infrastructure that enables it did not exist in prior eras.

Digital architecture can reproduce the structural problems
that United Pan Alta is designed to correct —
faster, and less visibly, than any prior form of power concentration.

Platform monopolization is the most immediate digital risk.

When a single platform controls the primary channel through which regional commerce, communication, or information flows, it acquires the structural leverage of a gateway controller — without the physical visibility that made historical gateway control politically contestable. A port that charges extractive fees is visible. A platform that deprioritizes interior node sellers through algorithmic design is not.

The effect is the same. The accountability is far lower.

Digital surveillance architecture presents a second structural risk. When one node deploys monitoring infrastructure across the digital interactions of other nodes—through platform dominance, hardware dependencies, or data collection agreements—it acquires an information asymmetry that translates directly into structural power. This is not hypothetical. It is already occurring across Northeast Asia in forms that the existing political frameworks are not equipped to address.

Artificial intelligence concentration presents the third and most long-term digital risk. The nations and corporations that control the foundational AI infrastructure of the region will shape its economic architecture for decades. If that control concentrates in one node — or in an external actor with no structural stake in regional balance — the cost distribution model of the Structural Pentagon becomes irrelevant. Power will have already been captured at a layer beneath the one the framework addresses.

The greatest structural threats
are those that operate below the level of political visibility.

United Pan Alta cannot be built on digital infrastructure that it does not understand. The current and coming generations cannot prepare a fair regional architecture if they allow the digital layer beneath it to be designed by those whose interests are not aligned with regional balance.

Vigilance in the digital layer
is not optional for those who care about the physical one.

The Generational Failure Scenario

There is a failure scenario that no external actor can impose.

It can only be chosen — quietly, gradually, and without awareness — by the generation this book is written for.

It is the failure of disengagement.

The digital world is extraordinarily effective at absorbing attention without producing structural awareness. Its systems are designed — deliberately, by people whose interests are served by the design — to maximize engagement and minimize reflection. The scroll is infinite. The notification is immediate. The reward is continuous.

A generation that is maximally engaged
and minimally aware
is the most easily governed generation in history.

The generational failure scenario for United Pan Alta is not dramatic. It does not involve war, collapse, or deliberate betrayal. It involves the slow accumulation of a generation that was present for the most consequential structural moment in Northeast Asian history — and was too distracted to recognize it.

Who consumed without contributing to the conceptual architecture their region needed.

Who shared without thinking about what they were building.

Who connected without asking whether the connections they were forming served the balance the pentagon requires.

The most dangerous failure is not opposition.
It is indifference dressed as participation.

This book cannot prevent that failure. No book can.

What it can do is name it clearly — so that those who read it cannot claim, later, that they did not know the stakes.

The digital generation has inherited a structural opportunity that no prior generation in Northeast Asia has possessed. The cost of cooperation has fallen. The tools of coordination exist. The conceptual framework is being prepared.

What remains is the choice.

History does not forgive the generation
that had every condition for preparation
and chose distraction instead.

But history equally rewards — quietly, without announcement — those who prepared when preparation was possible, who thought when thinking was unfashionable, and who built when building seemed premature.

This book is written for the second kind.

EPILOGUE

Leaving the Door Open - A Note to the Digital Generation

This book was written without urgency.

Urgency narrows judgment.
Narrow judgment hardens mistakes.

United Pan Alta was written to extend time, not compress it.

The most dangerous decisions are those made
when time is treated as an enemy.

What This Book Leaves Behind

This book does not leave behind:

- a program
- a mandate
- a blueprint for immediate action

It leaves behind:

- a shared reference
- a set of stable meanings
- a framework for preparation

What remains useful across generations
is rarely what is most loudly promoted.

On Unity

Unity is not an achievement to be claimed.
It is a condition that emerges.

When:

- cooperation costs less than conflict
- fairness reduces friction
- freedom remains protected

unity no longer needs to be demanded.

Unity that must be enforced
has already failed.

On Power

Power will continue to exist.
Competition will continue to exist.
Disagreement will continue to exist.

United Pan Alta does not seek to remove these realities.
It seeks to lower their cost.

Civilization advances not by eliminating power,
but by reducing the damage power can cause.

On Fairness

Fairness is not perfection.
It is not equality of outcome.
It is not moral consensus.

Fairness is the minimum architecture required for large systems to remain stable.

When fairness is absent,
no amount of strength is sufficient.

On Generations

This book does not belong to its author.

It belongs to:

- those who prepare without certainty
- those who choose without coercion
- those who inherit conditions they did not create

History moves forward
when responsibility outlives authorship.

What Remains Open

United Pan Alta is intentionally unfinished.

It must remain so.

Each generation will:

- reinterpret its meaning
- test its relevance
- decide its usefulness

A vision that cannot be revised
cannot survive.

Final Words

If this book is quoted,
let it be quoted for clarity.

If it is debated,
let it be debated for understanding.

If it is ignored,
let it be ignored until conditions change.

A good guidebook waits patiently
for those who are ready to use it.

This is where the book ends—
and where preparation begins.

A Note to the Digital Generation

This book has spoken across generations throughout its pages.

But this final note is addressed to one generation specifically — the current and coming digital generation — not because they are more important than those who came before, but because they are the ones who will decide whether this book was worth writing.

You were born into a world that was already connected.

You did not build the internet. You did not lay the submarine cables. You did not design the platforms. You did not negotiate the trade agreements that made cross-border commerce a daily routine rather than a diplomatic achievement.

You inherited all of it.

And yet — precisely because you inherited it rather than built it — you may be the first generation in Northeast Asian history that does not fully feel the weight of what it means to live in a connected region. Connection, for you, is not an achievement. It is a condition. It is the air you breathe, not the wall you climbed.

What is inherited without struggle
is easily taken for granted.

This book asks you not to take it for granted.

Patience in a Fast World

There is a tension at the heart of this book that has not been named directly until now.
This book is about preparation. About long horizons. About the kind of structural thinking that operates across decades rather than news cycles. About patience as a form of strength rather than a symptom of passivity.

You live in a world designed for the opposite.

The digital world you inhabit rewards speed. It rewards immediacy. It rewards the sharp reaction over the considered response, the viral moment over the durable idea, the engagement metric over the structural insight. Every system you interact with daily has been optimized — deliberately, by people who benefit from the optimization — to shorten your time horizon and intensify your present moment.

A shortened time horizon is not a personal failing.
It is an architectural feature of the world you were given.

This book cannot undo that architecture. It does not ask you to abandon the digital world or to pretend its rhythms do not shape your thinking. That would be neither honest nor useful.

What it asks is simpler and harder at the same time.

It asks you to hold two time horizons simultaneously.

The immediate one — where you live, work, create, and connect every day.

And the long one — where the consequences of today's structural choices will be felt by people who are not yet born, in a region that is still being shaped, by decisions that are being made right now, often without awareness of their structural significance.

The ability to hold a long horizon
while living in a fast world
is the defining capacity this moment requires.

It is not natural. It must be practiced. It must be chosen, repeatedly, against the current of a world that pulls in the opposite direction.

But it is possible.

And the fact that you are reading these words — to this point, in this book, which was never designed to compete with the infinite scroll — suggests that you already possess more of that capacity than the world around you has given you credit for.

What This Book Leaves With You

This book does not end with instructions.

It ends with a recognition.

The future of Northeast Asia will not be decided by governments alone, or by treaties alone, or by the outcomes of conflicts that have not yet occurred. It will be decided — quietly, incrementally, over decades — by the choices that ordinary people make about how to connect, what to build, whom to trust, and what kind of architecture to leave behind for those who come after them.

You are those ordinary people.

Not in spite of being young, digital, and connected.

Because of it.

The structural pentagon described in this book is not waiting for heroes. It is waiting for architects — people who understand that balance must be maintained rather than declared, that fairness must be built into systems rather than added afterward, and that the most consequential work is often the work that receives the least immediate recognition.

History does not always announce
the moment when preparation becomes legacy.

But it always remembers whether preparation was made.

This book was written so that you would have no excuse for not knowing the structure.

What you build within it — and what you refuse to allow to be built against it — belongs entirely to you.

The door this book opens
does not close behind you.
It waits.

— ✦ —

About the Author

Kyoungjoo Cha, known as Kenny Cha, was born in 1949 in South Korea and studied philosophy at Seoul National University, with a focus on the philosophy of human history. He is a writer and independent thinker focused on the structural forces shaping human societies. His work centers on the relationship between wealth, freedom, and fairness as the foundational architecture of durable civilizations.

Over several decades of international business activity and regional observation across Northeast Asia, he examined how geography, scale, power concentration, and economic design influence long-term stability. These experiences informed his conviction that sustainable strength depends less on dominance than on structural balance.

United Pan Alta applies this architectural perspective to Northeast Asia as a civilizational space. It is not a political project, but a directional framework grounded in geographic reality, economic logic, and generational responsibility.

— ✦ —

www.ingramcontent.com/pod-product-compliance
Lightning Source LLC
LaVergne TN
LVHW090527110826
845146LV00003B/1013

* 9 7 9 8 9 9 5 1 1 3 9 0 4 *